Tappity Tap Tap

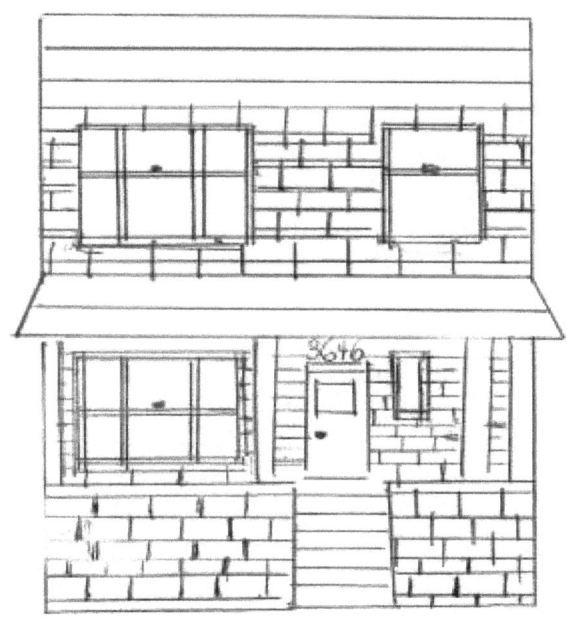

Nuggets of Gold

Written and Illustrated by
ROSALIE LOMBARDO

Copyright © 2020 Rosalie Lombardo
All cover art copyright © 2020 Rosalie Lombardo
All Rights Reserved
Second Edition
Original Publication Date – November, 2020

No part of this book may be reproduced or transmitted in any form or by any means, electronic or mechanical, including photocopying, recording, or by any information storage and retrieval system, without permission in writing from the author.

Cover Art – Rosalie Lombardo
Publishing Coordinator – Sharon Kizziah-Holmes

Paperback-Press
an imprint of A & S Publishing
A & S Holmes, Inc.

ISBN -13: 978-1-951772-78-9

AUTHOR'S NOTE

This is a true story November 2000, the week of what would have been my mother's eightieth birthday.

Dedication

Dedicated to the mothers of the universes who pass down their wisdom, yet seem doomed to be ridiculed and criticized by their offspring, until the time came when those mothers became spirits in the night. Only then did their children realize the annoyances and bothersome nudges were truly nuggets of gold. The offspring fortunate enough to recognize this gift unravel one of life's mysteries. Those who do not realize lose a great lesson.

Acknowledgments

My utmost gratitude and infinite love taps go to:

My brother, Calogero Lombardo, my first, last and in-between editor since the day I began writing stories. Thank you for a lifetime of direction and enlightenment.

Robert Mueller, my husband, for patience during the countless times I tapped his reserve of help while working on this book.

The mothers of this world who taught me that while under difficult circumstances and trying situations, they guide their children the best they are able.

My *spirit* mothers for endless guidance from the other side.

Special thanks for their insight to Susie Kuranishi and Nancy Dailey. Extra special thanks to Larry Cunningham.

"A tear dropped by."

Where did the thought come from? *A tear dropped by*. It held a strong presence like a dark scar burrowed deep in my skin yet raised above all other thoughts. *A tear dropped by.*

While facing the mirror, the strange words echoed through my mind. I dismissed the thought, but it came rushing back.

"A tear dropped by."

Why is this phrase commanding my attention?

Is there a message?

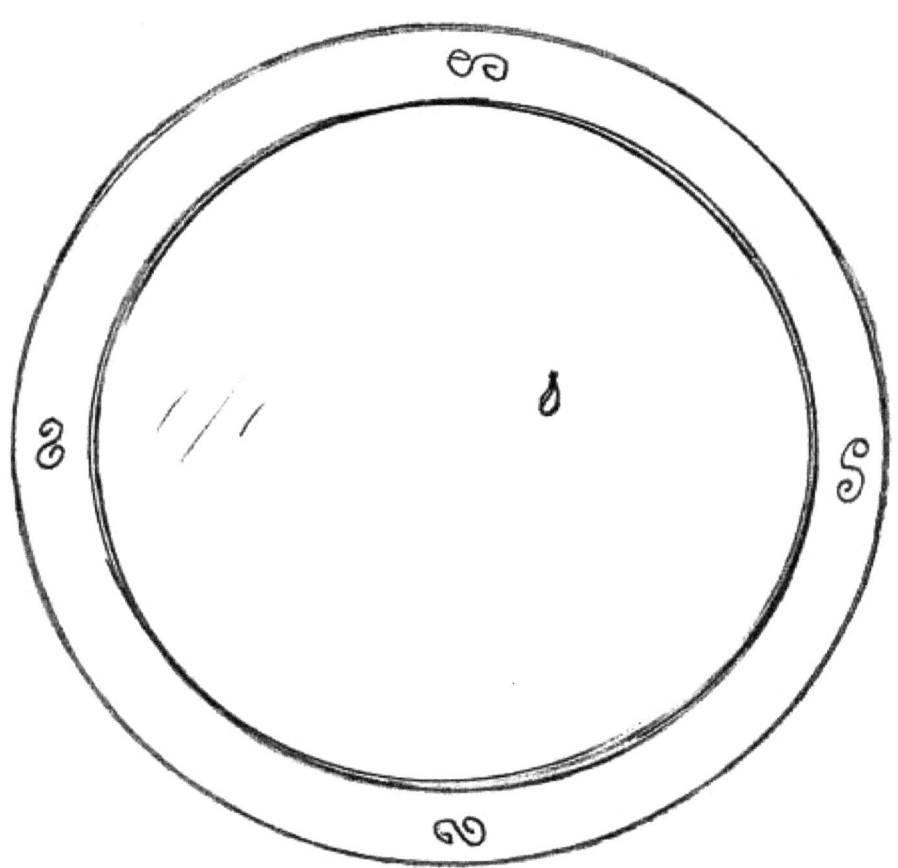

Then in my mind I heard *Tappity tap tap. Tappity tap tap. Tappity tap tap.* Without seeing her face, I knew it was Mom.

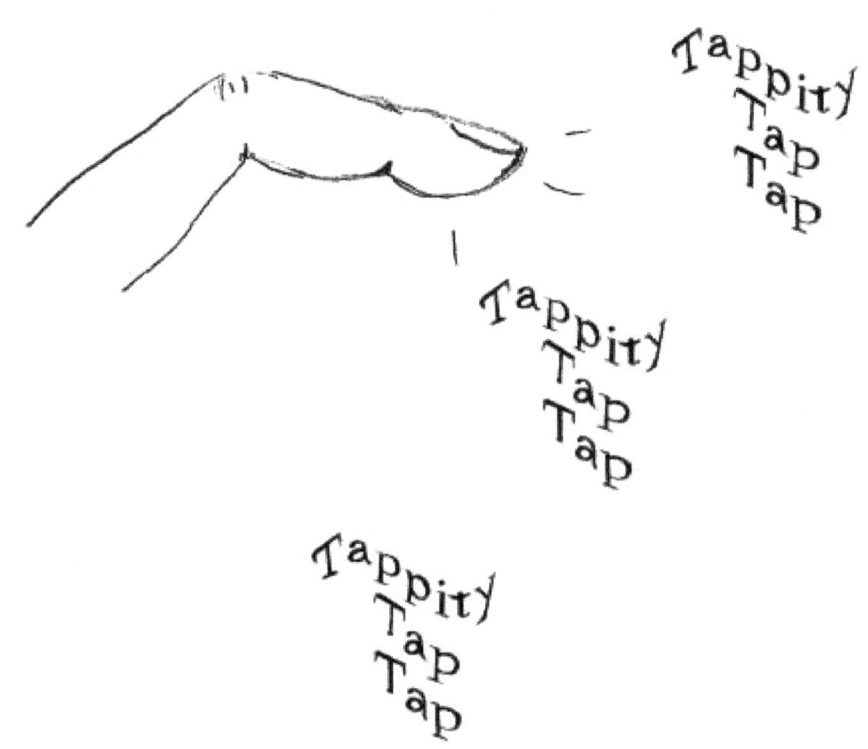

It became such a bothersome sound. I would hear that *tap tap tap* and the irritation would crawl up my spine. Couldn't she *tap* someone else? Please. The *Tapping* followed me everywhere:

    On the telephone – *Tappity tap tap*.

    At the door – *Tappity tap tap*.

    Through my mind in the middle of the day – *Tappity tap tap*.

    Even in my dreams, *Tappity tap tap*.

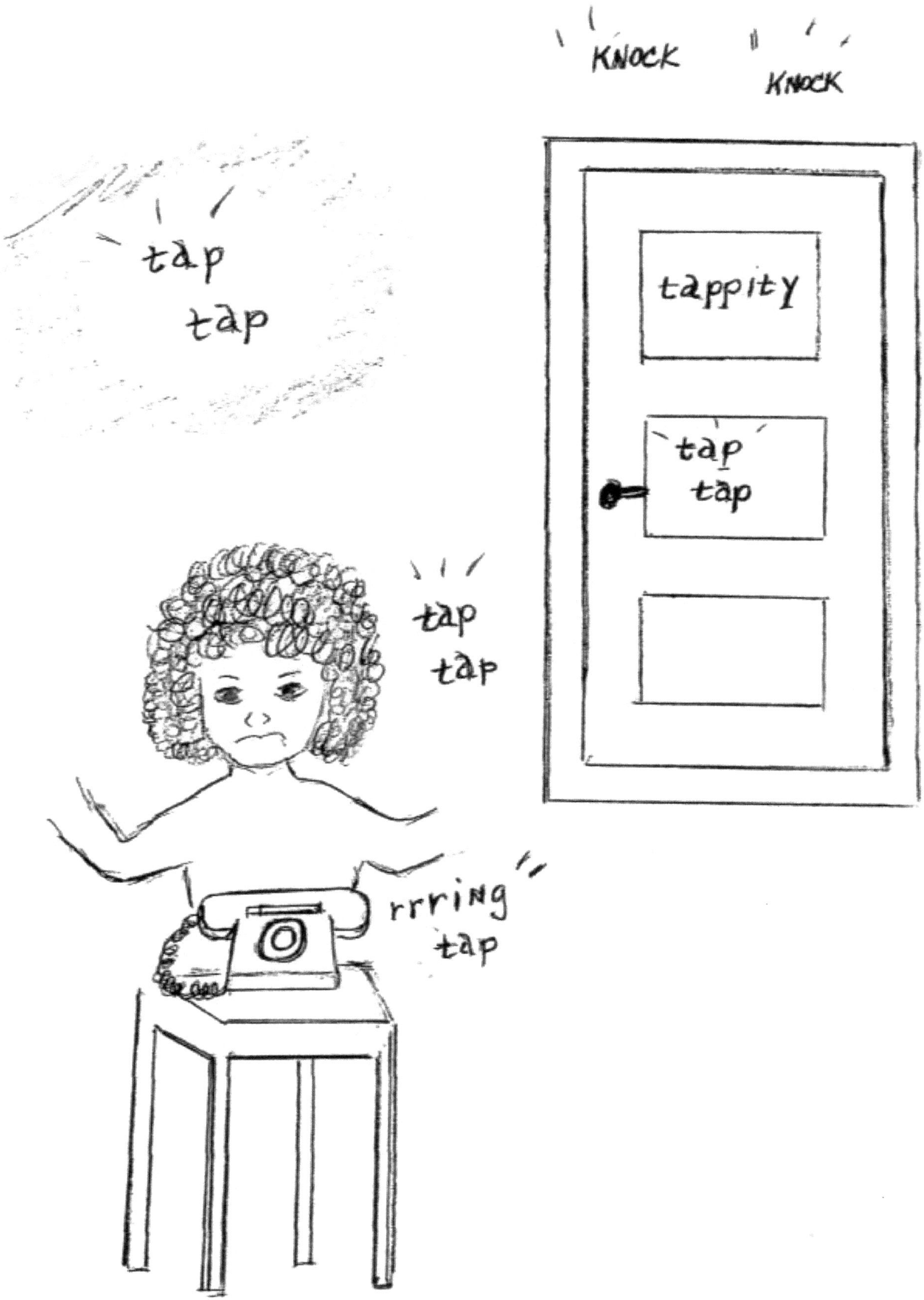
KNOCK
KNOCK
tap
tap
tappity
tap
tap
tap
tap
rrring
tap

I was always being *tapped*. *Tapped* to look at something; *tapped* to do something; *tapped* to take care of something; *tapped* to listen to something.

Tappity tap tap "Please take me to the store?"

Tappity tap tap "Will you go to a wedding with me?"

Tappity tap tap "Would you talk to your brother for me?"

Tap List

To Do

✓ 1) ~~pick up bread~~
✓ 2) ~~paint kitchen~~
✓ 3) ~~call contractor~~
✓ 4) ~~talk with brother~~
✓ 5) ~~bring home stamps~~
✓ 6) ~~write out checks~~
   7) escort mom to wedding
✓ 8) ~~pay phone bill~~
   9) pray

Then one day the *tap* was gone, and I was left here on my own.

For a while no *tap* was fine. Then sadness overwhelmed me.

Tappity would never return and neither would the *tap* nor the other *tap*.

Suddenly I longed to hear that *tap*.

I missed that *tap*. The *tapper* had died.

Leaving me to realize the *tapping* was no bother at all. Her *taps* were misconstrued, misunderstood. The *tapper* strived to teach me the best she could.

    I did not see what the *tapper* had tried to do for me.
And without warning the *tap* was gone. In its place,

    "a tear dropped by." Again.

    A lesson learned too late, I thought, so silently I cried.

One night from slumber I awoke to find her *tap* in full invoke.

  Tappity Tap Tap.

    TAPPITY TAP TAP.

      TAPPITY TAP TAP!

"Come," she said, "we have work to do. Stop sleeping on the job!"

This time I listened carefully, the *taps tapped* differently.
Taps of love, *taps* as guides; *taps* that teach from the other side.
   And there she was, amidst the Biggest *TAPPERS,* with a gigantic smile, glowing head to toe – a glimpse behind a secret door – her spirit came to teach me more.

Bring on the *taps* I hollered loud! I'll carry them out with *love* and *pride*! I won't rest 'til all is done! Give me more *taps*! I have room for more! Every *tap* I will adore!

I will distribute *taps* throughout the land and place them gently in my brothers' and sisters' hands.

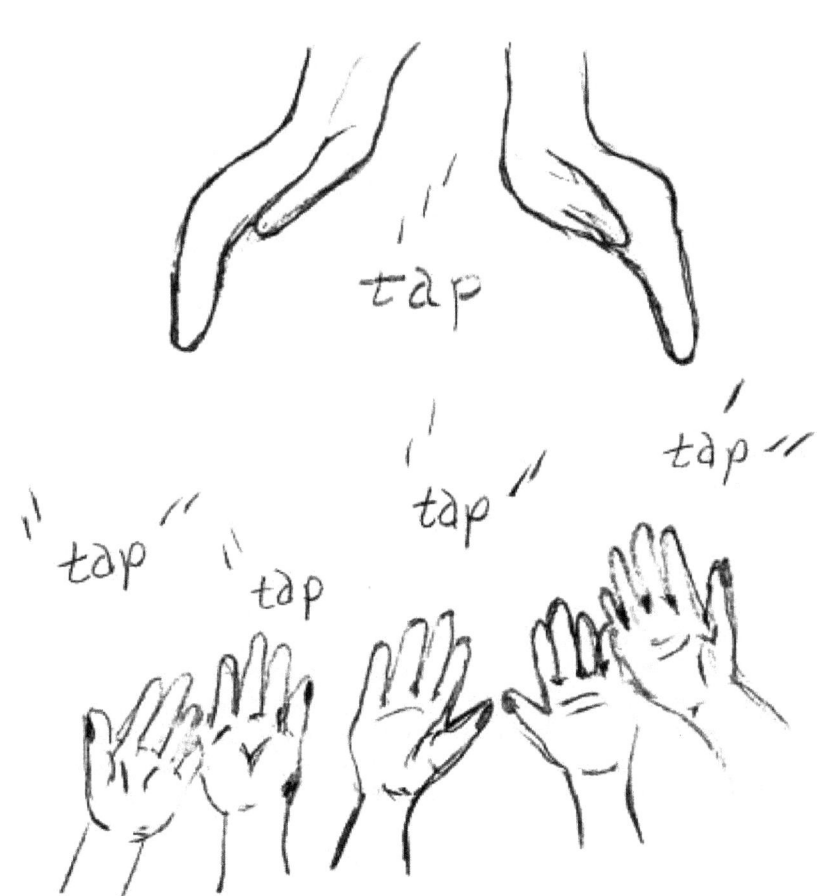

And from those *taps* I used to dread, a newfound awareness began.

Today I wait anxiously for sweet, sweet *taps* to come again to welcome them with open arms, with love and grateful honor.

I now understand what a treasure those *taps* really were. They were worth their weight in gold.

How lucky I am to be *tapped* all those years.

And ultimately, what a wonderful *Tapper* I, too, have become.

Tappity, tap, tap,

I love you mom

I Love You Mom

In memory of Mammè, (Maria Gioiacchina Bucaro Lombardo), my mother. Published on her 100th birthday, November 2020.

Her Spirit continues to tap me from the other side.

HAPPY BIRTHDAY MAMMÈ!

Eppi Birday Mammè

'Eppi Birday' {a family joke}

Peter Lombardo, grandson & Mammè on her 63rd birthday, November 14, 1983.

ABOUT THE AUTHOR

Rosalie Lombardo is an award-winning author. Her articles have been published in national and international periodicals and anthologies: Traveling in the Sixties, Creative Collections (Springfield Writers Guild) and Sleuths' Ink Mystery Writers. She was a featured columnist for a regional magazine.

Her love for diversity compels her to write in various genres. Her passion for children's stories inspired this picture book for adults.

Rosalie has taught classes in metaphysics, meditation, energy medicine, health and healing techniques throughout the United States.

She is a member of the International Society of Children's Book Writers and Illustrators, The Springfield Writers Guild and Sleuths' Ink Mystery Writers.

www.ingramcontent.com/pod-product-compliance
Lightning Source LLC
Chambersburg PA
CBHW041220240426
43661CB00012B/1097